Feel Me

WRITTEN AND ILLUSTRATED BY

AILY CARRANZA

SAN ANTONIO, TX

.

Edited by Kristen Corrects, Inc.
Author Photo, Cover Photo, Part 2 Interior Photos: Guillermo Velez
Cover and Interior Design by Adriana Cataño

ISBN: 978-1-953258-09-0

Library of Congress Control Number: 2025910336

First edition published 2025

Dedication

To Sunny, beloved giant Schnauzer and loyal friend,
May your love for the ocean's wonders never end.
September 5, 2023, your journey continued,
In our hearts your memory lives, forever drawn.

To my cherished husband,

My beloved, my soul's companion, my guiding star. In your presence, my heart soars to infinite heights. With every breath, I offer gratitude to the universe for the gift of our union, a sacred bond that weaves our souls together in an eternal dance. Your touch ignites a divine spark, melting fears and awakening the depths of my being. In your loving arms, I find my sanctuary, a haven where love, peace, and joy converge.

Together, our spirits entwine, creating a symphony of love that resonates across the expanse of time and space. Our love is a flame that burns with an otherworldly intensity, illuminating the darkness and guiding us through life's journey. It's a love that transcends the boundaries of the physical realm, speaking directly to the soul and awakening the deepest longings of our hearts.

You are my rock, my shelter, my sacred refuge, the missing piece that makes me whole. Your love is the missing beat that makes my heart and soul unfold, revealing the hidden harmonies of the universe. I am forever grateful for your presence in my life, for the gift of your love, your light, and your way.

As we embark on this new chapter, with the publication of this poetry book, I offer these words as a testament to our enduring love. May they be a reflection of the infinite beauty, the profound depth, and the unwavering commitment that we share. May our love continue to inspire, to heal, and to uplift all those who encounter it, and may it forever be the guiding force that illuminates our path, now and into eternity.

I love you more with each passing day, more with each breath, and more with each beat of my heart. You are the eternal valentine of my soul, the one who makes my heart sing, and my spirit soar. Forever and always, I'll love you, come what may, in this life and in all the lives to come.

Forever yours,
Aily

To my beloved children, my shining lights in this world,

As I prepare to share this collection of poems with the world, I am filled with gratitude and love for the two of you, who have been my constant source of inspiration and joy. You are the rhythm that makes my heart sing, the sunshine that brightens every day, and the safe haven where I can always find peace.

To my beautiful young woman, with a heart full of compassion and a spirit that soars, I dedicate these words to you. May they be a reflection of the love and pride I have for the incredible person you are becoming. May you always remember that you are strong, capable, and loved, and that your voice and presence in this world make a difference.

To my brave and curious young man, with a mind full of wonder and a heart of kindness, I offer these poems as a reminder of the boundless potential that lies within you. May they guide you on your journey, inspire you to chase your dreams, and remind you that you are never alone. May you always know that you are loved, supported, and cherished, and that your unique spirit is a gift to our world.

As I share these poems with the world, I do so with the hope that they will touch hearts, inspire minds, and bring people closer to the love and light that we all share. But most of all, I share them with you, my children, as a testament to our love, and as a reminder that you will always be the most precious and sacred part of my life.

May these words be a blessing to you, my dear ones, and may you always know that you are loved, not just for who you are, but for who you are becoming. May your paths be guided by love, wisdom, and compassion, and may your hearts always be filled with joy, peace, and wonder.

With all my love, now and forever,

Mom

To my dad, Jose Luis, my best friend and protector for eighteen years, my greatest guardian angel: Thank you for all you taught me, for your guidance, for the bear hugs, the long talks, for your love, and especially for your light. See you in my dreams, feel you in my heart, love you, Daddy.

To my readers, Where there is faith and love accompanied by hope, nothing—absolutely nothing—is impossible! If I could heal, so can you! As hard as it gets, don't give up because I assure you the fight for your life is the only fight that's most definitely worth fighting for!

To my doctors, mentors, teachers and healers: Thank you, thank you, thank you! Much love and light to all!

Aily Carranza

Author's Note

As I sit down to write this author's note, I am filled with a mix of emotions: sadness, gratitude, and hope. In the fall of 2023, I lost my beloved companion, Sunny, my black giant Schnauzer who was more than just a pet—he was my best friend, my confidant, and my soulmate.

Named after the sun for his warm heart and brightness, Sunny was a constant source of comfort and joy in my life. For almost a decade, he was by my side, sharing in my joys and sorrows, and offering me a sense of safety and security that I had never known before.

As someone who has survived child abuse, family tragedy, kidnapping, sexual assault, and cancer, I have learned to navigate the darkest of times and find a way to heal and thrive. But losing Sunny was a different kind of grief, one that shook me to my core and made me realize how much he had become a part of me. I rarely go to the beach anymore, a place that was once our safe haven, where I could sit and meditate with my eyes closed, knowing that Sunny was by my side, watching over me.

Despite my best efforts to stay strong, the pain of losing Sunny has been overwhelming at times. As a neurodivergent person with autoimmune thyroid disease, I have to work hard to maintain my mental, physical, and spiritual health. But Sunny was more than just a companion—he was my rock and my creative partner. I could tell him anything, and he would listen with a wisdom and understanding that was beyond words.

I remember the day we brainstormed together on the beach in Port Aransas, Texas, in February 2022. My husband and son had driven us to our favorite spot, and as we walked along the shoreline at sunrise, I would recite words from my heart, and Sunny would howl joyously as if to say, "Yes, yes, yes! This is it!" It was as if he had a deep understanding of the creative process, and he would always let me know when I was on the right track.

Sunny had a special place in his heart for the ocean and its creatures, and his favorite sea creatures were dolphins, whales, and octopuses. He would always perk up whenever we saw them, and I could sense his excitement and wonder.

Five months after his passing, I finally felt ready to let go of my old boy. I spread a towel on the sand, placed his urn in the middle, and surrounded it with rose incense and pink rose petals. As I released his ashes into the ocean, I felt a sense of peace wash over me, as if the cosmic mother was embracing him and letting me know that he would be safe and never alone.

In that moment, I knew that I had to title this book Feel Me, a phrase that Sunny and I would often share on our walks along the beach. It was a phrase that spoke to the deep connection we shared, a connection that went beyond words and spoke to the very heart of our being.

These poems were written with so much love, in honor of Sunny, and the rest of the poems are for you, so you can feel me, so you can feel the love, the joy, and the connection that Sunny and I shared. But I also wrote these poems so you can feel and be inspired by the immense love and light in my heart and soul.

As I look back on our time together, I am reminded that even in the darkest of times, there is always hope, always a way to heal and thrive. If I can heal, you can too. If I can thrive, so can you. These words are not just a mantra, but a testament to the human spirit, which is capable of overcoming even the most daunting challenges.

As you read these poems, I offer my deepest gratitude to the universe for the gift of Sunny's presence in my life, and for the lessons he taught me about love, loyalty, and the interconnectedness of all beings. May his spirit continue to guide me, and may his memory inspire you to cultivate compassion, kindness, and courage in your own life. May we all remember that we are never alone, that we are always connected to each other, to the natural world, and to the divine. And may we always feel the presence of those who have touched our hearts, guiding us toward healing, growth, and transformation.

The following is the elegy for Sunny:

OCEAN'S ELEGY: A TRIBUTE TO SUNNY

In twilight's hush, where sea meets sky,
A majestic soul now sails on by,
Sunny, dear, your pawprints fade,
Yet memories linger, an eternal shade.

Your heart was bound to ocean's roar,
Where dolphins leapt and whales explored,
With every wave, your spirit took flight,
In harmony with sea's celestial light.

In dreams, I see you, wild and free,
Chasing sea sprites, wild with glee,
Your fur aflame with sunset's fire,
As blue angels rise, your soul's desire.

One emerges, radiant, from the deep,
A feminine form, in mystic sleep,
Her wings, a shimmering cascade,
Guiding you home, through eternal glades.

Together, you sway, beneath the tide,
Where sea and sky entwine, side by side,
In cosmic rhythm, your hearts now beat,
Forever roaming, wild and sweet.

Though your physical form may fade,
Your essence merges with ocean's jade,
In every wave, your spirit plays,
Eternal companion to sun-kissed days.

Rest now, dear Sunny, in celestial peace,
May the ocean's whispers guide your soul's release,
In memories, your love shines bright,
A beacon in darkness, pure delight.

PART I

Echoes of the Ocean

Dolphins

With wise and ancient eyes, they gaze,
Into the depths of the ocean's haze.
Their secrets and stories, a gold mine,
A wisdom and knowledge sent from the Divine.

Their clicks and whistles, a language of old,
A legacy of learning, to be told.
Their playful leaps, a celebration, too,
Of the mysteries, that only they know true.

Moonlight Serenade

Under the moon's silver glow
Dolphins gather, in a shimmering row
Their sonic signals a celestial song
Echoing through the waves all night long

Their sleek bodies, a glimmering band
Gliding through the sea, hand in fin
Their playful bursts, a choreographed dance
In harmony with the lunar trance

Their echolocation, a symphony of light
A nocturnal serenade in the moon's pale sight
Their world, a dreamland, of sea and sky
Where dolphins reign, and magic meets the eye

A Playful Dolphin

In the ocean's waves, a splash of fun,
A dolphin soars beneath the sun.
Its fin slices through, with a graceful glide,
As it plays and frolics with a joyful stride.

With a twinkle in its eye and a grin so wide,
It swims and bursts with a playful pride.
It chases schools of shimmering fish
And races the waves with a laughing wish.

Its mystic chatter echo through the sea
As it communicates with a language so free.
A symbol of joy, and a heart so light,
The dolphin plays in the ocean's delight.

The Underwater World

Beneath the waves, a world unfolds,
Where dolphins reign in watery gold.
The sunlight filters, in shimmering rays,
Illuminating realms in a mystic haze.

Corals bloom in vibrant hues,
A colorful landscape for dolphins to cruise.
Schools of fish, in sparkling arrays,
Dart and weave in a mesmerizing display.

Sea fans sway in a gentle breeze
As dolphins glide with effortless ease.
The ocean floor, a tapestry so fine,
A world of wonder where dolphins entwine.

Their sonic signals echo through the sea,
A masterpiece of communication, wild and free.
In this underwater world they play and roam,
A magical domain where dolphins call home.

Arctic Angels

In icy waters, a sight to behold
Beluga whales, with hearts of gold
Their white skin glistening, like snow in the sun
Their playful antics, a joy to be done

With gentle smiles and curious eyes
They swim and play in the Arctic's disguise
Their melodic bursts, a symphony so sweet
A language of love that can't be beat

Their graceful movements, a ballet so fine
A testament to their beauty, and their divine
In the frozen north they reign supreme
A true marvel of the ocean's dream

Dolphins' Language

In the ocean's depths, a language shared,
Dolphins converse, with creatures bared.
With whales they speak in low, rumbling tones,
Exchanging secrets beneath the waves' thrones.

With fish they chat in rapid clicks and beeps,
Coordinating hunts in a synchronized sweep.
Sea turtles, too, receive their friendly calls,
As dolphins guide them through the ocean's halls.

Even octopuses, with their clever minds,
Engage in playful banter with dolphin kind.
Their conversations a wondrous, underwater dance,
A harmonious exchange in the ocean's trance.

While we may not fully understand their talk,
Dolphins' social nature is truly a marvel to balk.
Their language skills, a testament to their grace,
A shining example of oceanic embrace.

A Dolphin Learning from a Wise Old Sea Turtle

In the ocean's heart, a lesson prevails
As a dolphin listens to a turtle's wise tales.
The turtle shares its secrets so old,
Of the ocean's rhythms, and stories untold.

The dolphin learns of patience and pace,
Of the importance of finding its own space.
It discovers new ways to navigate the sea,
And how to respect the creatures that be.

The turtle teaches of the dangers below,
And how to avoid the ocean's hidden woe.
The dolphin absorbs this knowledge so true,
And thanks the turtle for lessons anew.

With a nod of gratitude and a flick of its fin,
The dolphin swims on with new wisdom within.
For in the ocean's deep, a learning curve unfurls
Where creatures of all kinds can share and swirl.

Dolphins' Daybreak

As sunrise splashes the ocean's face
A pod of dolphins takes its place
In the waves' hold, they sway and play
Their chirps and trills heralding a new day

With graceful leaps, they greet the dawn
Their shadows mirrored on the water's pond
Their fins slice through with gentle might
As they frolic in the morning light

Their echolocation, a masterpiece of sound
A harmonious hunt beneath the waves profound
Their world, a wonderland of sea and sky
Where dolphins reign, and magic meets the eye

The Dolphins' Lullaby

In the ocean's cradle, a dolphin lies
Swaying to the waves' gentle sighs
Its underwater opus a soothing refrain
A lullaby, to ease the pain

Of the world above, where waves crash strong
And the winds howl loud all day long
But here in the depths, all is calm and still
Where the dolphins' song can heal and thrill

So rest, little one, in this watery space
And let the dolphins' lullaby fill the space
With dreams of the sea and all its grace
And wake to the dawn, in a dolphin's place.

The Beluga's Lament

On the Arctic chill, I sing my song
A melancholy tune that's been sung all day long
I roam the icy seas in search of prey
But the waters are warming, and my home is fading away

My once-pristine habitat, now scarred and gray
The ice that cradled me is melting away
I swim through the noise of humanity's din
And wonder if my kind will ever win

But still I sing, in the darkness and cold
A beluga's lament, for a world that's grown old
For though my heart aches and my future's unsure
I'll sing of the beauty that once was pure.

A Dolphin's Family

In the ocean's heart, a family thrives,
A pod of dolphins, bound by love and lives.
The mother guides with wisdom and care,
Her calf beside her, playful and fair.

The father watches with strength and might,
Protecting his family through day and night.
The aunts and uncles play and teach,
Sharing secrets in their underwater speech.

Together they swim in harmony and grace,
Their mystic chatter a joyous grace.
They hunt and play in the ocean's expanse,
A family united in a watery trance.

Their love and trust, a shining light,
A flare in the depths, a guiding sight.
For in the dolphin family, we see
A reflection of love, wild and free.

Dolphins Making Love

Amid the waves a tender scene unfolds,
As dolphins mate, their love stories told.
Their sleek bodies entwined in a graceful embrace
In the ocean's darkness, a passionate, underwater place.

The male's fin curves, a gentle caress,
As he guides his mate in a loving possess.
Their song of the sea, a sweet serenade,
A language of love, in a watery glade.

Within the pod, a bond forms strong and true,
As the couple's love forever shines through.
Their union a celebration of life and the sea,
A testament to nature's beauty, wild and free.

In the heart of the sea, a new life begins,
As the dolphins' love, a precious gift within.
Their love story, a story carved in gold,
A shining jewel in the oceans unfold.

A New Life Born

In gentle waves, a miracle unfolds,
As a mother dolphin, her baby enfolds.
Within her womb, a new life grew,
Nurtured by love and the ocean's hue.

With a gentle push and a soft sigh,
The calf emerges into the world's light.
The mother's gaze, a warm grace,
As she welcomes her baby to the dolphin race.

The calf's first cry, a tiny sound,
Echoes through the waves, a joy profound.
The mother's love, a guiding light,
As she nurtures her young, through day and night.

With each passing moment, the calf grows strong,
And in the ocean's arms, their bond will last long.
A beautiful beginning, a new life bright,
In the gentle waves, where the dolphins take flight.

Dolphins Converse

In watery realms, a language reigns
Where clicks and whistles convey meaning's stains
Dolphins converse, in a world apart
Their communication, a work of art

With frequency shifts and pitch so fine
They weave a tapestry of sound divine
Their chatter echoes through ocean's space
A concerto of intelligence and grace

They speak of food, and where to find
Of social bonds that intertwine
Of playful jumps, and ocean's grace
In a language rich with emotional pace

Their chirps and trills, a code so true
A language unique, as they communicate anew
A world beneath, where sounds unfold
The dolphins' language, a story to be told.

Octopus

In secret depths, an octopus's lair
Eight arms interweaved, a curious air
They change color, shape, and guise
To communicate with wistful eyes

They mate, they frolic, they play, they hide
Their social bonds, like tentacles, abide
Cooperating, hunting, side by side
In an underwater world, they reside

With intelligence, they solve and thrive
Their social behavior, a wonder alive
A cephalopod's charm, we can't deny
A glimpse into their world, and we ask why

Can we learn from their adaptable grace?
Embrace change, like the octopus's chase?
For in their social behavior, we see
A beauty that's both wild and free.

Dolphins' Slumber

In the ocean's embrace, they rest
Their dreams, a mystery, forever guessed
Their bodies float in a gentle sway
As they sleep in a world far away

Their minds, a whirlpool, of thoughts untold
As they process the secrets they've been told
Their underwater symphony, a lullaby sweet
As they drift off to a peaceful retreat

Their sleep, a refuge from the ocean's roar
A time to recharge, and dream some more
Their slumber deep, a mystery to share
As they sleep with no care

Their dreams, a window to their soul
A glimpse of wonder, beyond control
Their sleep, a gift from the sea above
A reminder of the beauty, of their love.

A Mother Dolphin and her Newborn Heart

A tender tale of love so true,
A mother dolphin and her calf, anew.

In ocean's waters, a birth takes place,
A tiny soul with fins and grace.

The mother's gaze, a warmth so deep,
As she beholds her newborn sleep.

With gentle nuzzles, she guides the way,
Teaching her calf to swim and play.

With each passing day, the calf grows strong,
And in its eyes, a wisdom shines so long.

Together they swim in the ocean's grace,
A bond so fierce, a love in place,
A testament to nature's gentle art,
A mother dolphin, and her newborn heart.

Dolphins at Play

Flippers flutter, fins frolic,
In the waves, a playful romp.
Dolphins sway with joy so bright,
Their laughter echoes through the ocean's light.

With seaweed garlands they play hide-and-seek,
And chase the schools of fish so sleek.
Their sonic signals a merry tune,
As they frolic beneath the sun's warm boon.

In the waves' hold they twirl and spin,
Their playfulness, a fortune to win.
With every leap, a splash of glee,
Dolphins at play, a sight to see!

A Dolphin's Intelligence

In the depths, a mind so keen,
A thinking creature, with thoughts unseen.
Dolphins ponder, with a brain so bright,
Solving problems with insight and might.

With echolocation, they map the sea,
A mental image of the world they see.
They learn and teach, with a memory so grand,
A culture shared across the ocean's land.

Their intelligence, a wonder to behold,
A mirror to ours, a story to unfold.
They communicate in a language so fine,
A world of thought beyond our own design.

With curiosity, they explore and play,
A never-ending quest for knowledge each day.
Their intelligence, a gift so rare,
A gem to cherish, beyond compare.

Flippers and Finns

In the ocean's playground, they frolic and spin,
Their laughter echoes, a joyful din.
With seaweed garlands, they dance and play,
Their antics mischievous, in a sun-kissed way.

They chase the waves and leap with glee,
Their splashing games a sight to see.
They surf and somersault, with a grin so wide,
Their playfulness a treasure to abide.

With bubbles and clicks, they create a show,
A spectacle of fun for all to know.
Their fins entwined, they spin and twirl,
In an underwater ballet, so full of whirl.

In the ocean's murk, they find delight,
Their playfulness, a wondrous sight.
So let us marvel at their joy so true,
And cherish the magic that dolphins do.

Dolphins in the Moonlight

Silver light upon the sea
Dolphins swim, a lunar spree
Their sleek forms, glowing bright
In the moon's gentle, ethereal light

They leap and splash, a shimmering sight
Their acoustic signals, a celestial delight
As they play in the moon's embrace
Their grace and beauty, a wondrous place

Their shadows sway upon the waves
A mystical, dreamlike, moonlit cave
Where magic reigns, and wonder roams
In the moonlit realm of dolphins' homes.

A Dolphin's Glee

In ocean's openness, they play and glide,
Their sleek forms shining, as they frolic and ride
The waves, with grace and ease, they dive and slide,
Their clicks and whistles echoing, a joyous tide.

With intelligence and love, they roam the sea,
Their hearts as deep as the ocean's mystery,
Their powerful bursts, a testament to glee,
A sight to cherish, a wonder to see.

Their fins, a gentle wave, as they swim by,
Their eyes, a window to a world beyond the sky,
Their beauty, a gift that touches the heart's sigh,
A pearl to behold in this world's disguise.

As sun sets low, they lead their pod away
From shore's hold, to depths of the ocean's gray
Their whispers echo, as they dive and play
In darkness vast, where secrets come to sway

Their lights a beacon in the darkening sea
Guiding their kin through mystery and glee
Their hearts a compass to the unknown's key
A map to hidden worlds, where magic comes to be

And as they swim, the stars above them twinkle
A celestial guide to their eternal sprinkle
Their journey on, a tale of wonder and twinkle
A story told, in whispers, to the ocean's wrinkle.

A School of Dolphins

A shimmering wave, a silver tide,
A school of dolphins, side by side,
Their fins, a flutter, as they play,
Their rippling vibrations, a joyous sway.

With graceful leaps, they sway and glide,
Their forms a blur as they swiftly ride,
The ocean's waves, a gentle space,
A home, a haven, a place of grace.

Their curiosity, a guiding light,
Exploring depths, both day and night,
Their playful hearts, a prize to see,
A wonder, a magic, wild and free.

Together they roam, a shining band,
A school of dolphins, hand in fin,
A testament to unity and love,
A fortune sent from above.
In pods they gather, a social band
United in play, in hunt, in stand
Their mystic chatter, a language so fine
A masterpiece of friendship, a bond divine

They swim in tandem, a harmonious glide
Their fins entwined, a ballet inside
They help each other, in need or in play
A brotherhood of fins, a lifelong way

Their young ones learn, from elders so wise,
The ways of the sea and social guise
They form close bonds that last a lifetime through
A testament to friendship, pure and true

In their social world, a hierarchy reigns
But kindness and play ease any pains
For dolphins know that unity is key
To a life so rich, in love and glee.

Dolphins Dance at Sea

With joyful jumps, they dance on the sea
Their playful spirits, wild and free
They chase and splash, in a frolicsome spree
Their laughter echoing, a contagious glee

They surf and slide, on waves so bright
Their antics a delight, a wondrous sight
They play with seaweed, a silly game
Their fins entwined, a playful flame

With bubbles and clicks, they create a show
A spectacle of fun, for all to know
Their playfulness, a splendor to uphold
A gift from the sea, a story to be told

In their playful world, they frolic and spin
An underwater world, a joy to win
For dolphins know that play is the key
To a life of happiness, wild and carefree.

Fin and Fiona

In the turquoise depths, a tale unfolds,
Of Fin, a dolphin, with a heart of gold.
He swam the seas in search of his mate,
Until he met Fiona, his soulmate so great.

Their eyes met in a sparkling glance,
And Fin knew at once, she was his second chance.
Fiona's smile lit up the ocean's face,
And Fin's heart skipped a beat in a playful race.

They swam together, side by side,
Their sonic signals a sweet glide.
They chased the waves and swayed in the tide,
Their love so strong, it could not be denied.

Fin showed Fiona the ocean's hidden gems,
And she revealed her secrets, in sweet dolphin whims.
Their love grew stronger with each passing day,
And in each other's fins they found their way.

One moonlit night, in a lagoon so still,
Fin proposed to Fiona, with a shell so thrilled.
She said yes, with a splash and a grin,
And their love story became a legend within.

Now Fin and Fiona swim hand in fin,
Their love forever, in the ocean's heart within.

A Whale's Melody

In the vast blue darkness, a voice does resound,
A whale's deep bass, a rumble all around.
A haunting melody that echoes through the sea,
A concerto of longing, wild and carefree.
With each moan and murmur, a story does unfold,
Of secrets hidden in the depths untold.
A language ancient, yet timeless as the tide,
A whale's lullaby that the ocean does provide.

In the silence of the deep, its voice does reign,
A king of the abyss, with a song so pure and plain.
A call to the unknown, a hymn to the blue,
A whale's eternal song, forever echoing anew.

A Dolphin's Intellect

In depths profound, a mind so keen
Aware and alert, a thinking machine
The dolphin's brain, a wondrous sight
Processing thoughts, with speed and might

With problem-solving skills, they adapt and thrive
In a world of waves, they survive and strive
Their memory sharp, a vast, storied sea
Recalling paths and secrets of the deep

Their language complex, a symphony so fine
A chorus of clicks, a tale divine
Communicating thoughts with grace and poise
A sophisticated mind that never knows noise

With self-awareness, a rarity in the wild
A consciousness that's hard to be defiled
Their intelligence shines like a beacon bright
A marvel of nature, a wonder in sight.

A gentle mother, a guiding light
A young one by her side, a precious sight
She nuzzles close, a loving embrace
Teaching ways of the sea, with a tender grace

With playful leaps, she shows the way
To hunt and swim in a sun-kissed bay
Her calf watches, with eyes so wide
Drinking in knowledge with a curious stride

Together they swim through waves so blue
A bond so strong, a dream come true

The mother's wisdom, a guiding force
Shaping a future with a gentle, loving course

As the sun sets, in a golden glow
They rest together, in a peaceful flow
The mother's heart, full of love and care
For her young one, a prize beyond compare.

The Ocean's Acrobat

On the open sea they play
Their laughter echoing, in a joyful way
They chase and splash, in a watery game
Their fins entwined, in a playful frame

With seaweed strands, they create a scene
A playful drama, in a watery dream
They leap and twirl, with a carefree grace
Their playfulness in a wondrous, underwater place

In the ocean's lap, they frolic and spin
Their playful antics, a gem to win
They surf and slide on waves so bright
Their laughter ringing in a joyful delight

With bubbles and clicks, they create a show
A playful spectacle for all to know
Their playfulness, a gift from the sea
A treasure trove of wonder and glee.

A Dolphin's Light

In the morning light, they rise to play
Their sleek bodies, a shimmering array
They leap and splash, in a sparkling spree
Their joyful voices a symphony

With the sun's warm touch, they frolic and glide
Their playful spirits, a wondrous tide
Their song of the sea, a language so bright
A world of wonder, in a dolphin's light

Two of a Kind

In the ocean's chill, a bond so strong
A friendship formed, where hearts belong
Two dolphins swim, side by side
Together they glide in a watery stride

Their clicks and whistles, a language so true
A conversation shared between two
They play and leap in a joyful space
Their friendship a pearl, in a dolphin's place

Through waves and tides, they stand as one
A bond so unbreakable, beneath the sun
Their hearts entwined, like seaweed in the sea
A friendship so true in a dolphin's glee

Together they roam in a world so wide
A friendship so strong, it cannot subside
A testament to love, in a dolphin's heart
A bond so true, a work of art.

In ocean's embrace, a bond takes shape,
Between two dolphins, a lifelong escape,
Their fins entwined, a friendship so true,
A bond so strong that ocean's depths renew.

Together they swim through waves so bright,
Their laughter echoes, a joyful delight,
They jump for joy in a synchronized spin,
Their friendship a fortune, a heartfelt win.

With rippling vibrations, they share their tale,
A language of love that never will fail,

Their hearts so pure, their spirits so light,
A shining example of friendship's might.

Through tides and storms, their bond remains strong,
A testament to love that never goes wrong,
Their friendship a flare that shines so bright,
An illumination for all to take flight.

So let us cherish this bond so rare
And honor the friendship that dolphins share,
For in their hearts, we find a truth so true,
That friendship and love forever shine through.

A Dolphin's Family Bond

In the ocean's arms, a family resides
A pod of dolphins, with love inside
Their fins interlaced, a tender hold
A bond so resilient, a family to behold

The mother guides, with a gentle pace
Her calf beside, a smile on his face
The father watches, with a steadfast gaze
A protector true, in a dolphin's ways

Together they swim through waves so bright
A family united in a watery light
Their underwater symphony, a language so dear
A family's love, without fear

They play and leap, in a joyful ring
A family's bond, that will always cling
Through generations, their love will flow
A dolphin family, forever to grow.

Dolphin Loyalty

In the ocean's deep, a loyal heart beats strong
A dolphin's love, forever true and long
They form their bonds with a steadfast might
A loyalty so fierce, a guiding light

Through waves and tides, they stand as one
A loyal companion until the end is done
They protect and care, with a selfless grace
A loyal friend in a dolphin's embrace

Their pod is family, a loyal tribe
Together they roam through oceans wide
Their loyalty unwavering, a steadfast creed
A bond so strong that will forever proceed

Through generations, their loyalty will shine
A flare of hope, a heart so divine
A dolphin's loyalty, a prize so rare
A gift so precious, beyond compare.

A Whale's Song of Sorrow

In the depths of the ocean, a whale does mourn
A song of sorrow, a heart that's torn
A melody of longing, a tale of woe
Echoes through the waves, a story to be told

With each moan and murmur, a tear does fall
A concerto of sadness, standing tall
The whale's voice trembles, a pain so true
A lament for what's lost, a heart that's bruised anew

The song speaks of separation, of loved ones gone
Of oceans vast and empty, where once they'd swum
It whispers of regret, of moments left behind
A haunting reminder of a sorrow so unkind

In the darkness of the deep, the whale's song resides
A monument to heartache, where tears abide
A reminder that even in the ocean's space
Sorrow can find a voice, a space to fill the place.

A Watery Wonderland of Play

In sun-kissed waves, they frolic and play,
They leap and soar in a joyful way,
With jumps and splashes, they dance and spin,
Their playful spirits, a wondrous win.

With seaweed strands, they weave a game,
A watery wonderland where they proclaim
Their joy and laughter, a contagious delight,
An underwater utopia, in the ocean's light.

Their melodic bursts, a sonata so bright,
A language of play that fills the light,
With bubbles and waves, they chase and race,
Their playful hearts, a wondrous, sun-kissed place.

In the ocean's world, they find their glee,
A world of play, where they can be free
Their playful souls, a star so bright,
A gift from the sea, a pure delight.

Interminable and Selfless Love

In deep waters, a love so true,
A dolphin's heart beats just for you,
Their gentle eyes, a window to the soul,
A love so white that makes the heart whole.

With graceful leaps, they show their devotion,
A love so deep, like the endless ocean,
Their playful touch, a tender caress,
A love so deep, that never will repress.

In their embrace, we find a peaceful place,
A love so warm that fills the space,
Their resonant echoes a sweet serenade,
A love so true, that never will fade.

With every breath, they show their care,
A love so selfless that's beyond compare,
Their love for each other, a shining light,
A sign of hope in the darkest night.

So let us learn from these loving friends,
To love with all our hearts, until the end.

A Dolphin's Cleverness, an Astonishing Sight

In the ocean's depths, a mind so bright
A dolphin's intellect, a wondrous sight
With problem-solving skills, they navigate with ease
And learn with speed, like a swift-moving breeze
Their memory is sharp, their thoughts so clear
They communicate in clicks, a language so dear
They recognize themselves in a mirror's gaze
A sign of self-awareness, in a world of daze

With creativity, they play and explore
Using tools and tactics to hunt and store
Their social bonds, a complex network so fine
A testament to intelligence that shines so divine

Their curiosity, a driving force so strong
They investigate and learn all day long
In the saltwater, a mind so bright
A dolphin's intelligence, a wondrous sight.

Dolphin's Grace

On the wide ocean, a vision so fair,
A dolphin glides, with grace beyond compare.
With fluid motion, she slices through the sea,
A shimmering form of beauty and glee.

Her dorsal fin, a crescent moon so bright,
Cuts through the waves with gentle might.
Her playful dives, a masterpiece so free,
A ballet of joy for all to see.

With eyes so wise, and heart so kind,
She swims through life with a peaceful mind.
A true ambassador of the ocean's grace,
A dolphin's beauty in every place.

A Whale's Song of Joy

In the deep blue waters, a whale does sing
A song of joy, a heart that takes wing
A melody of delight, a tale so bright
Echoes through the waves, a joyful sight

With each click and whistle, a smile does spread
A symphony of happiness, in every whale's head
The song speaks of wonder, of ocean's grace
A celebration of life, in a whale's place

In the sunlit waters, the whale's song resounds
A chorus of joy that echoes all around
A reminder that even in the deep blue sea
Joy can swim alongside, wild and carefree!

Dolphin Love Pod

In the ocean's heart, a family resides,
A pod of dolphins, with love inside.
The mother guides with a gentle pace,
Her calf beside, a smile on his face.

The father watches with a steadfast gaze,
Protecting his family in a world of waves.
Siblings play in a splashing grace,
A tight bond in a watery place.

Together they swim, through sunlit seas,
A family united in a world of ease.
Their sonic signals, a language so true,
A family's love, in a dolphin crew.

With every leap, a story unfolds,
Of love and trust, in a family's hold.
In the deep blue, a family resides,
A pod of dolphins, with love inside
As the sun sets, the pod gathers 'round,
Sharing stories of adventures underground.
Young ones listen, wide-eyed and aglow,
As elders recount tales of the ocean's flow.

Auntie Delphinia tells of a shipwreck's gems,
Uncle Finley shares his famous "fish-leap" measure.
Cousin Luna describes a coral reef's delight,
While Granny Whiskers whispers secrets of the night.

The stars appear, like diamonds in the sky,
As the dolphins' laughter echoes, wave to wave, high.
The reunion continues through moonlit sea,
A celebration of family, wild and free.

Whispers of the Past

In days of youth, I gazed upon the sea
Where dolphins played, wild and carefree
Their fins sliced waves, like silver knives
As they danced and leapt, with joyful lives

Their chirps and trills echoed through the air
A language of love, beyond compare
I watched in awe as they swam by
Their grace and beauty left me shy

Summer sunsets saw them frolic and play
In waves that glistened, like diamonds in array
Their laughter echoed, as they chased the tide
Their joy so real, my heart could not hide

Now years have passed, and I've grown old
But memories of dolphins remain forever bold
Their whispers linger in my heart's ear
A nostalgic tale of a love so dear

Ah, dolphins of youth, how I miss your grace
But your memory stays in this nostalgic place.

Splashing Joy

On sun-kissed waves, they dance and play,
Their laughter echoes in a joyous sway.
With fins interlaced, they leap and spin,
Their playful splashes, a concerto within.

They chase and race, in a frolicsome delight,
Their clicks and whistles a joyful, sparkling light.
They surf and dive, with a grin so wide,
Their playful spirits a wondrous, oceanic pride.

With bubbles and waves, they create a show,
A spectacle of joy, for all to know.
Their playful energy, a pearl to see,
A celebration of life, wild and free.

So let us marvel at their playful grace,
And bask in the joy of their watery place.
For in the dolphins' play, we find our own delight,
And a sense of wonder that shines so bright.

A Dolphin's Social Grace

In pods they gather, a family so fine,
Their bonds so strong, their hearts so divine.
They swim together, in the ocean's waters,
Their social grace, a wondrous place.

They play and leap in a synchronized spin,
Their acoustic signals, a language within.
They help and care for each other's young,
A community so tight, where love is sung.

They share their secrets in a whispered tale,
Their social fabric, a story so frail.
But strong it stands in the ocean's might,
A testament to their social delight.

So let us be amazed at their social ways,
And learn from their love, in these oceanic days.
For in the dolphins' pod we see a shining light,
A beacon of hope, in the dark of night.

Unbreakable Leaps of Love

In deep waters, a dream come true,
Dolphins' hearts, a love so clean and new.
Their fins entangled in a tender embrace,
Their love shines bright in the ocean's place.

With mystic chatter, they speak of love,
Their language sweet, a language from above.
They care and nurture, with a gentle touch,
Their love so strong, it can heal and clutch.

In playful leaps, they show their delight,
Their joy so contagious, it shines so bright.
With loyalty and trust, they stand as one,
Their love so unbreakable, under the sun.

In their pod, they teach us to love,
To cherish and honor, from above.
For dolphins know the secrets of the sea,
And their love is a gift, for you and me.

A Dolphin's Heart

A dolphin's heart beats with a gentle grace,
A symbol of love in a vast, watery space.
It pumps a current of kindness and care,
A never-ending stream of compassion and repair.

With every beat, a wave of empathy flows,
Connecting souls, like ripples on the ocean's rose.
It holds a deep wisdom, born of the sea,
A knowing that all living things are meant to be.

In its chambers a gentle melody plays,
A song of unity that echoes through the days.
A dolphin's heart is a fortune so rare,
A shining example of love compare.

A Pod

In ocean's depths, a family strong,
Dolphins bond, where love does belong.
Their pod, a circle, tight and true,
A loyalty that forever shines through.

Through waves and tides, through sun and storm,
They swim together, never to be torn.
Their hearts entangled, in a lifelong vow,
To stand as one, through the sea's eternal brow.

They care for young, and guide them on,
Teaching ways of the ocean's song.
They nurse the sick and comfort the sad,
In a loyalty that's never bad.

Through jumps for joy, through a laugh and a sigh,
Their bond endures, until the day they die.
For in the pod, they find their home,
A loyal family, where love is grown.

But when a member wanders, lost at sea,
The pod sets out, to search for thee.
They scan the waves, with eyes so bright,
Until the lost one is back in sight.

With resonant echoes, they welcome home
The wanderer, who had strayed alone.
They guide him back to the family fold,
With a love so strong, it never grows old.

For though the ocean may be vast and wide,
Their bond is stronger, and will not subside.

Their loyalty, a light in the deep,
Shines bright and true, in the darkest sleep.

And so the pod, once more complete,
Swims on together in a harmonious beat.
For in their hearts, a loyal love resides,
A love that's pure and never divides.

Dolphins' Love Guide

In ocean's heart, a love that's blue,
Dolphins' devotion shines anew.
Their fins interweaved, in tender hold,
A bond so strong, that never grows old.

With gentle nuzzles, they show their care,
And in each other's eyes, a love so rare.
They swim together, in harmonious grace,
A testament to love, in every dolphin's face.

Their playful surges, a joyous display,
A celebration of love, every single day.
With melodic bursts, they sweetly say,
"I love you more, with every passing bay."

In dolphins' love, we find a guide,
A shining example to abide.
For their love is pure and true as can be,
A treasure trove for you and me.

Through waters vast, they journey side by side,
Together facing the rising tide.
Their friendship deep, a secret to unfold,
A shining light that never grows cold.

In dolphins' friendship, we find a truth,
That love and loyalty are forever youth.
For in their hearts, a special place,
They hold the key to a lifelong grace.

Dolphins' Graceful Movements

With fluid grace, they glide through the sea,
Their bodies sleek, in effortless ease.
Their fins and flippers, a gentle sway,
As they navigate the ocean's way.

Their movements flow like a river's stream,
A sonata of motion, a dream.
They leap and dive, with precision and poise,
Their beauty mesmerizing, as they unfold their joys.

In their graceful movements, we find a peace,
A sense of harmony in the ocean's release.
For in the dolphins' grace, we see a truth,
That beauty and elegance are a natural youth.

Beluga Momma

On icy waters, a gentle space,
A beluga mother cradles her young with grace.
Her milky-white skin, a nursery soft and bright,
A haven for her calf in the Arctic's pale light.

With tender clicks, she guides her little one
Through frigid seas, where their bond has just begun.
She teaches and protects with a loving fin,
Their bond a gem, in the ocean's wintry kin.

Together they swim, in a frozen dance so fine,
A testament to love in the harshest of climes.
For in the beluga's heart, a mother's love resides,
A warmth that melts the ice is where their love abides.

Heart of the Ocean

In the ocean's heart, they swim and play
Their laughter echoing, in a joyous way
They race and chase, in a watery game
Their playful hearts, a prize to reclaim

With each leap and splash, they show their grace
Their playful souls, a wondrous, underwater place
Their joy is contagious, it spreads so wide
A world of happiness in a dolphin's stride.

A Beluga's Song

In the depths of the ocean, a melody flows,
A beluga's song, a masterpiece that glows.
A series of clicks, a chirping serenade,
An underwater concert, in an icy shade.

With vocal cords that vibrate, a tune so clear,
The beluga sings without a single fear.
A language all its own, a whistle in the dark,
A haunting melody that echoes through the spark.

In the Arctic silence, its voice rings out so bright,
A beacon of beauty in the frozen night.
A song of joy and wonder, a tale of the deep,
A beluga's serenade in the ocean's endless sleep.

G rowing up as the child of someone who was murdered deeply affects your emotional development. Grief, like many other things in life, can be seen as a skill—one that never truly leaves you. But if you learn how to navigate grief in a healthy way, it can become a source of strength, helping you grow into a more compassionate and loving person.

When I lost my father to murder as a teenager, I didn't know how to process it. My grief overwhelmed me, taking a toll on both my body and mind. It wasn't a healthy way to cope. But, decades later, Sunny's death changed the way I understand and handle grief. His passing gave me the chance to reshape my pain into something healing—something I could carry with me as a life skill. Yet instead of mourning from a place of deep hurt, I chose to honor Sunny's memory by transmuting the energy of sorrow into nurturing energy. I allowed peace to reign in my heart by painting Angelic or Divine creatures. When Sunny was still with us, he enjoyed watching me paint.

Throughout the grieving period, I felt Sunny's spirit by my side as I created the following illustrations. I chose to place them after the poems to honor Sunny without distracting from the rhythm of the words. I hope you enjoy this collection.

Aily's Heart

June 12, 2022

The Goddes under the Full Moon

September 17, 2024

Protection

May 2022

Sunny's Vortex

November 11, 2024

Goddes of Unconditional Love

October 2023

Mother Peace

September 25, 2024

Peace

September 12, 2024

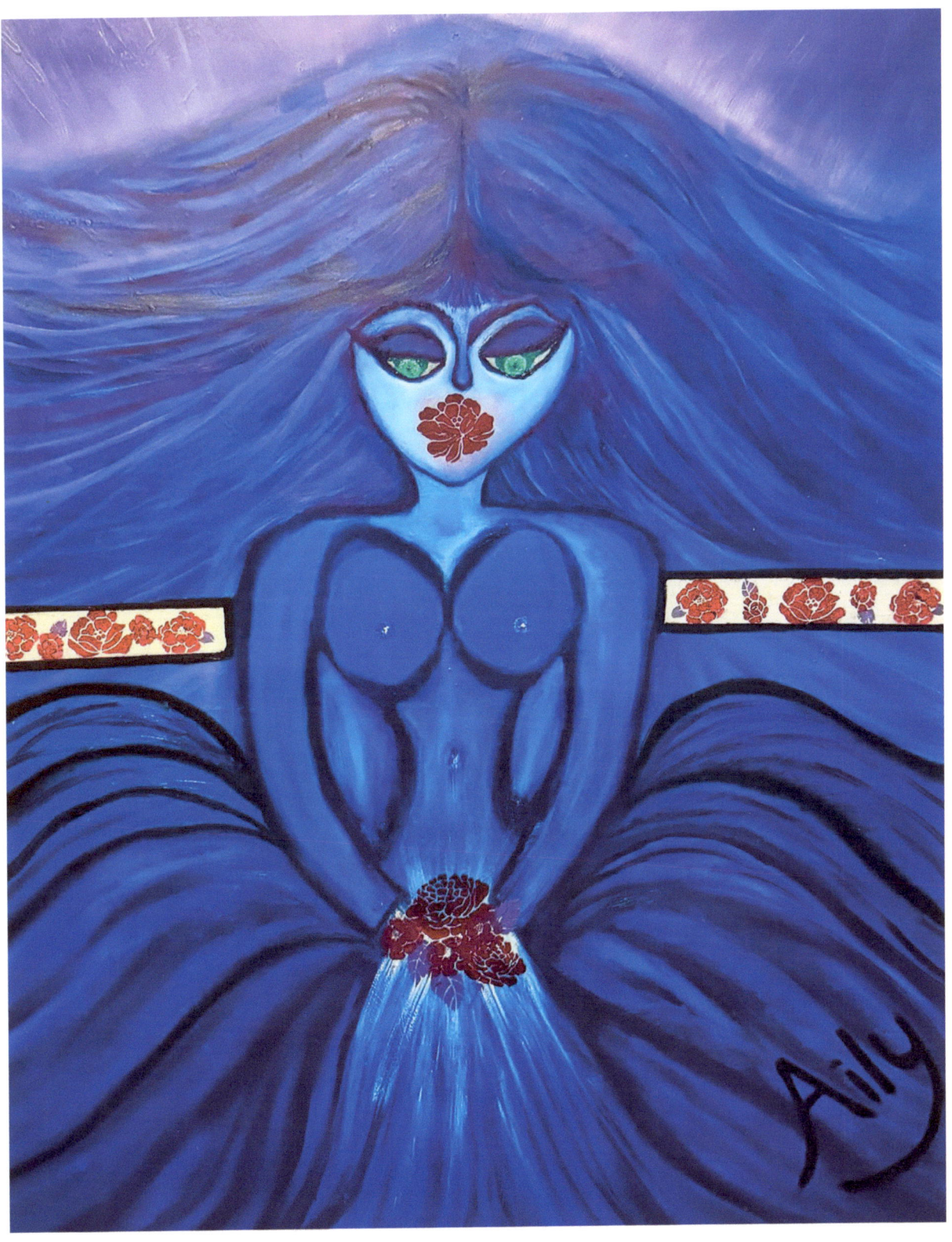

Blue Creature of Divinity

December 20, 2024

Blue

Januaty 9, 2022

PART II

Rising Tides, Rising Spirit

Rising Tides, Rising Spirit is more than a collection of poems—it's a living tribute to the healing power of love, nature, and spirit. Each verse reflects pieces of my personal journey through grief, loss, motherhood, and transformation. Sunny, my beloved Schnauzer, was not just a pet but a soul companion whose presence guided me through some of life's most sacred and sorrowful passages.

Through the tides of deep pain and the light of inner awakening, I've found solace in the divine feminine, the ocean's mystical rhythm, and the resilience of the human heart. These poems are my offering—to anyone seeking connection, comfort, or the courage to rise from their own depths and remember that they, too, are made of stardust, seawater, and strength.

I hope this collection resonates with you.

Under the Moon's Pale Light: A Tribute to Sunny

As the moon casts its silvery glow,
I feel your absence, dear Sunny, and know,
You've transitioned to the Rainbow Bridge above,
Where ancestors await, with endless love.

Your howls, a symphony of joy and delight,
Echo in my heart, a bittersweet refrain tonight,
Your ginormous body, a bundle of silky black fur,
A gentle giant, with a heart so pure.

I miss our meditation sessions under the moon's pale light,
With you by my side, I felt the universe's delight,
Your presence, a reminder of the interconnectedness of all,
A sense of oneness that transcended the physical wall.

Your kisses, a language of love, that spoke directly to my soul,
A reminder of the deep bond we shared, a love that made me whole,
Through milestones and memories, you were always by my side,
A constant companion, a loyal friend, a love that would not subside.

As I grieve, I know that you're free,
Running wild with the ancestors, wild and carefree,
Your spirit, a spark of the divine, now merged with the cosmic sea,
A droplet of love that's returned to the source, wild and free.

Yet even in death, your love remains,
A flame that burns, a heart that still sustains,
The memories we made, the laughter, the tears,
A legacy of love, that dispels all fears.

So I'll hold on to the memories, dear Sunny, of our time together,
And know that your love will forever be my shelter,

In the stillness of the night, I'll feel your presence near,
A gentle nudge, a whispered reminder, that you're always here.

As I look up at the moon, I'll know that you're watching over me,
A guardian angel, a spirit guide, a love that's set free,
And though you're no longer by my side in physical form,
Your love, your spirit, will forever be my norm.

Rest now, dear Sunny, and run wild and free,
May your journey be filled with joy, love, and ecstasy,
And know that I'll always love you, and cherish the memories we made,
A bond of love, that will forever be displayed.

From Darkness to Light: A Mother's Prophecy

On twilight's hush, where life and death entwine,
A miracle unfolded, heart and soul aligned.
Twenty-one hours of labor's sacred design,
A baby girl, a blessing, pure and divine.

In first embrace, she found my loving breast,
A blissful moment forever etched in rest.
Yet, fate's dark veil soon shrouded my sight,
As lifeblood ebbed, and death's cold whisper took flight.

Flatlined, I heard a whisper, clear and bright,
"A son shall come; your ovaries hold the light."
Years passed, and prophecy unfolded its might,
A son, a love, a family, bathed in golden light.

Through darkness and sorrow, I emerged anew,
A soul revived, a heart reborn, a love shining true.

A Modern-Day Fairytale

In shadows' gentle hush, where fate's dark veil lifts high
Our love story unfolded, a legendary gift from the sky
A chance encounter, summer's warmth ignited the flame
1988's poolside party, where love's spark took its first name

Yet, fate's mysterious hand had woven our threads before
A Texas beach, summer '83, our hearts secretly adored
Five years passed, and our love's flame burned bright and true
Until the whims of fate struck, and our hearts were torn anew

Mid-spring '92, our unborn son's loss did we mourn
Seventeen and nineteen, our love faced its darkest dawn
Then, '93's tragedy befell, my father's life slipped away
And we, two lovers, parted, in sorrow's dark decree to stay

In distant lands, we wandered, lost, yet love's ember glowed
I, in pursuit of truth, and you, in academic's noble woe
Until '94's darkest night, when terror's grip held me tight
And you, my love, my lifeline, were the first I called, in desperate plight

Two years passed, and '96's cruel fate bound me fast
To a loveless marriage, born of violence, forever to last
A daughter born, a product of pain and shame
Yet, you, my love, adopted her, and gave her your name

Then, 2003's rescue, when you, my love, played your part
Together we rose, against all odds, our love conquered fear and heart
In 2005's promise, we found our home, our love persevered
A son was born, our family complete, our hearts now fully cleared

With Sunny, our beloved Schnauzer, by our side
Our giant, gentle friend, our love for him did not subside

Together we shared laughter, tears, and life's delight
A family bound by love, in all its beauty and light

Thus, our love story stands, a modern-day fairytale, told
A tale of love's triumph, over fate's dark veil, forever to unfold.

The Ocean Fairy

In the depths of turquoise twilight
Where sea and sky interlace
A gentle soul stirs, ethereal and kind
The Ocean Fairy, a vision divine

Her hair flows like seaweed, soft and green
Her voice, a soothing melody, a siren's dream
She emerges from the waves, a shimmering form
A guardian of peace, a heart that's warm

With wings like a manta ray, she glides
Through the darkness, a radiant light inside
Seekers of solace, she finds and guides
And whispers secrets of the ocean's tides

In her embrace, the weary find rest
Their souls, like sea glass, polished and blessed
Their hearts, like shells, filled with her gentle song
A lullaby that echoes all day long

She weaves a tapestry of tranquility
With every wave, a thread of serenity
A mystic dance, beneath the starry sea
The Ocean Fairy, a spirit, set free

Aqua Goddess Rising

On the depths of sapphire silence
A shimmering form begins to surface
A mermaid's essence, pure and radiant
Unfurls like a lotus, petals of luminescence

Her hair flows like the ocean's currents
Golden locks that shimmer, like sunlit torrents
Her voice, a melodic whisper, a gentle breeze
That stirs the soul and awakens the heart's seas

With every flick of her iridescent tail
She weaves a spell that entrails
The magic of the ocean's darkest night
And the luminescence of its shimmering light

Her aqua essence, a concerto of blue
Echoes the heartbeat of the universe anew
A goddess rising from the waves below
A symbol of power, in the ebb and flow

In her depths, a wisdom that's ancient and true
A knowing that's born from the ocean's womb anew
A reminder of the magic that lies within
A call to embrace the mystery and the spin

With every wave, a whisper, a gentle hue
A reminder of the goddess that shines through
A mermaid's essence, a symbol of the sea
A reflection of the magic, that's meant to be free

A Tapestry of Triumph

In the depths of my soul, a story unfolds
Of trials and tribulations, of wounds that would not grow old
A survivor of family tragedy, I bore the weight of grief
A burden that threatened to consume me, to steal my belief

But I refused to be defeated, to be silenced by pain
I rose up, a phoenix from the ashes, my spirit unbroken and unstained
I walked through the fire, and emerged, transformed and renewed
My heart, once heavy with sorrow, now soars, with a spirit anew

My body, a temple, weathered by life's storms
A uterus lost, a gallbladder gone, the scars of Hashimoto's form
But I have learned to tend to this temple, to nurture and to heal
Through my journey as a health and wellness coach, I've learned to reveal

The interconnectedness of body, mind, and spirit, I now know
A holistic approach to wellness, that honors the wholeness of me, I've come to show
I've walked the path of self-discovery, of growth and of transformation
And emerged a butterfly, with wings outstretched, in all my formation

The loss of my beloved Sunny, my giant Schnauzer, dear friend and guide
Touched the depths of my sorrow, and summoned me to step inside
The grief that I had long suppressed, the wounds that I had yet to mend
I faced them, head on, and allowed myself to descend

Into the depths of my own heart, where love and sorrow entwine
I found the courage to confront, to heal, and to redefine
My relationship with myself, with my body, with my soul
I emerged, reborn, with a heart that's whole

Today, I stand, a testament to the human spirit's might
A woman, weathered by life's storms, yet radiant, in the light

I am a tapestry of triumph, woven from threads of pain
A story of resilience, of hope, of the human spirit's capacity to sustain

In Truth and Light, all things are Divine
A wisdom that guides me, on this journey of mine
In peace I stand, for the Kingdom of Love lives within my heart
A sanctuary of compassion, where love and forgiveness never depart

In this sacred space, I've found my strength and my voice
A place of healing and transformation, where love is the only choice
And so I rise, a woman transformed, with a heart full of love
A tapestry of triumph, woven from the threads of my soul, sent from above.

In Yemaya's Arms

In life's most turbulent hours, where sorrow's waves did crash
I clung to Yemaya, Mother of the Sea
Her gentle arms, a refuge from life's rash
Embracing me, in compassion's ecstasy

Her whispers calmed the tempests of my soul
As I navigated life's turbulent, dark role
With every breath, I felt her love made whole
In her vast ocean, my heart found its goal

Through trials and tribulations, I held tight
To Yemaya's wisdom, shining like a light
In her celestial song, I found my own voice bright
An opus of hope, in the dark of night

Yemaya, Orisha of the Deep Blue Sea
Forever in my heart, your love shines bright and free.

Ocean's Mystical Embrace

In the depths of cerulean vastness
Lies a realm of wonder, beyond the human grasp
A world of mystery, where secrets unfold
A tapestry of magic, woven with threads of gold

The ocean's essence, a concerto of blue
Echoes the heartbeat, of the universe anew
A rhythm that whispers, ancient truths untold
A melody that stirs the soul's deepest gold

Within its waves, a wisdom that's timeless and true
A knowing, that's born, from the depths of the blue
A whisper of magic that dwells deep inside,
A beckoning to embrace the mystery and glide.

In its darkness, a light that shines like a star
A beacon that guides through the depths of the scar
A symbol of hope, in the darkest of nights
A reminder of the magic that ignites

The ocean's lair, a mystical hold
A place where dreams unfold, where secrets are told
A realm of enchantment, where magic is real
A world of wonder that the heart can feel

The Goddess Within Me

In sacred depths within, a goddess shines,
A radiant light that guides me through life's strife,
A spark of divinity that forever mine,
A sign in the darkness, a heart alive.

Through trials and tribulations, she's refined,
Purified by fire, strengthened by each test,
Her wisdom whispers secrets, soul to mind,
A gentle breeze that soothes, a love that's best.

With every breath, I feel her presence near,
A comforting hold that banishes all fear,
Her grace illuminates the path I tread,
And in her loving eyes, my heart is fed.

This inner goddess, a reflection true,
A symbol of my strength, my spirit anew.

Within my soul, a Native American goddess reigns,
White Buffalo Calf Woman, wise and kind,
Her spirit guides me on an enlightened path,
A journey of service, for the greater good aligned.

With every step, I walk in harmony,
With Mother Earth and all her creatures, I entwine,
My heart beats for the land, the skies, the sea,
A sacred unity, where love and respect divine.

Through trials and tribulations, I've been refined,
My faith in Divinity, a flame that still shines bright,

A beacon in the darkness, a light that's mine,
A gift to share with others on this sacred night.

With sage and sweetgrass, I'll walk this path anew,
A goddess within me, a spirit that's true.

Fairy Goddess

Within my heart, a fairy goddess plays,
With purple pixie dust, she spreads her grace,
A sprinkle of magic, a twinkle in her sway,
Transforming trials into wonder, a wondrous race.

Her heart overflows with gratitude and light,
A purple soul that shines, a light in the night,
For she has faced the darkness and emerged anew,
In a realm of whimsy, a paradise, both fresh and true.

In this enchanted land, she frolics, free and wild,
A heaven on earth, where love and joy are piled,
Her spirit soars on wings of sparkling dew,
A fairy goddess, living magic, pure and true.

With every breath, she whispers thanks and praise,
For the magic that surrounds her, in endless, shimmering ways.

The following poems are inspired by my adverse childhood experiences.

Unbroken Spirit

In the crucible of suffering, I found
A spark of resilience, a soul unbound
From the shackles of trauma, I broke free
And rose, a phoenix, in the light of destiny

•

A Child's Courage

In innocence betrayed, I found a strength
A courage born of trust, in the divine length
Of a soul that knew, despite the darkest night
A light would guide me, to the dawn's early light

•

Shattered Trust

Trust, like a mirror, shattered on the floor
Reflecting the fragments of a soul once more
But in the shards of brokenness, I found
A glimmer of redemption, a love profound

•

Resilience Born

From the ashes of trauma, a new creation rose
A resilience born, of the divine that knows
No bounds, no limits, to the soul's deep might
A radiant butterfly, unfolding its wings in light

Silence Broken

The silence was a chrysalis that held me tight
A cocoon of secrets that kept me from the light
But I broke free, and found my voice, my song
A melody of liberation that echoed all day long

•

Healing Journey

The journey to healing was a labyrinth of the soul
A path that wound through shadows, to the light that makes me whole
With each step forward, I found my heart's deep core
A wellspring of compassion that healed me, evermore

•

Unshackled

I broke free from the chains of trauma's heavy weight
And found my own liberation, in the light of love's pure state
I rose up, unafraid, and claimed my rightful place
And in my freedom, found a peace that time and space won't erase

•

Voice of Courage

My voice, once silenced, now rings out clear and strong
A voice of courage, that speaks out, righting the wrong
I share my story, to help others find their way
And in my truth, I find solace, come what may

Rising Above

Above the ruins, of a childhood lost and torn
I rose, like a lotus flower, in a beauty reborn
I transcended the trauma, and found my inner peace
And in my heart, a love that will forever release

•

Triumphant Soul

My soul, once battered, now stands triumphant and tall
A warrior's spirit that has faced the worst of all
I've walked through the fire, and emerged refined and pure
A shining testament to the strength that I endure

A Love So Strong

In soft, golden light, where shadows play
Our love story unfolded, in a bygone day
A chance encounter, summer's warmth did ignite
Our hearts, forever entwined, in love's sweet delight

Our families, like Montagues and Capulets of old
Did bear a grudge, a feud that would not grow cold
But we, like star-cross'd lovers, did defy
The hatred and the anger, that sought to deny

Our love, a flame that burned, so bright and true
In secret, we did meet, our hearts beating anew
We'd steal away, to gardens, where the night blooming flowers
Did bloom, and in their scent, our love found its powers

But fate, it seemed, did conspire against our love
And in the end, it was our hearts that did rise above
For though our love was forbidden, it did set us free
And in its memory, our hearts forever will be.

Through Trials and Tribulations

Through life's turbulent hours, we stood as one
Together facing challenges beneath the golden sun
Our bond, forged in the fire of adversity's might
Emerging stronger, our love, a bright light

Like Jenny and Oliver, in love's pure delight
We cherished every moment, in the fleeting light
Of life's uncertain journey, where shadows frolic and play
Our love shone bright, a beacon, to guide us on our way

Through hospital halls, where darkness oft did reign
My love, my husband, stood by me, through joy and pain
With every test, every trial, our love did find a way
To overcome, to rise above, in a brighter, loving day

His endless love, a flame that burned pure and bright
Illuminating my path through the darkest, endless night
With him by my side, I knew I'd face no fear, no test
Together, our love would find a way to forever rest.

Sacred Mother Goddess within Me

Within my soul, a sacred mother goddess shines,
A sign of hope, a heart that's strong and divine,
A love that's fierce and boundless, like a lioness's might,
A protector of her cubs, through day and endless night.

When death and darkness threatened, you refused to yield,
Your spirit unbroken, your will, a shining shield,
You nourished a girl's life, despite the pain, the staples, and the scar,
A testament to your strength, a love that went far.

Against all odds, a miracle unfolded in time,
A son, a blessing, a gift, a heart that entwines,
Your love, a flame that burns bright, a illuminating light,
A trust in the Divine, a faith that takes flight.

You are a guardian, a warrior, a sacred mother true,
A reflection of the goddess in all that you do.

Unbroken Spirit

My heart, once heavy with sorrow's weight
Now soars, with a spirit unbroken and great
Through life's refining fire, I found my inner strength
A resilience born, of love's transformative length

Like a lotus flower that blooms in muddy waters
I rose above the pain, and found my spiritual daughters
My divine family, a sacred gift from above
A father, mother, daughter, and son, bound by unconditional love

With Jesus as my guide, I walked the path of redemption
And found my own sacred family, in this life's new creation
Together we thrive, in love's pure light and delight
A bond of gratitude that shines, like a beacon in the night

In this divine family, I've found my peaceful nest
A sense of belonging, where love forever rests
My heart, once broken, now healed and made whole
A testament to love's power, that forever makes me soar.

The Cosmic Mother

In life's darkest moments, where heartache's waves did roar
I clung to the Cosmic Mother, celestial arms that enfold and clash
Her gentle grace, a refuge from life's rash
Embracing me, in compassion's ecstasy and splash

Like a child, I nestled in her loving care
Drinking from the cup of her divine, merciful air
Her presence, a balm to my soul's deepest wound
A healing that flowed, from her heart to mine, unbound

In her cosmic womb, I found solace and peace
A sense of oneness, with the universe's release
The stars, the moon, the sun, all sang in harmony
A celestial chorus that echoed her sweet melody

With every breath, I felt her love, her light, her way
Guiding me through life's labyrinth, night and day
The Cosmic Mother, a beacon, shining bright and true
Illuminating my path, and forever seeing me through.

Rebirth

From ashes of suffering, I rose anew,
A phoenix of faith, where darkness once dwelled.
My thyroid reborn, like a butterfly's cue,
Transformed, I emerged, my spirit unveiled.

Hashimoto's chains broken, conditions fled,
Cancer's shadow lifted, health restored to me.
Through trials, I found strength in my inner bed,
A goddess awakened, wild and carefree.

With every breath, I claimed my divine right,
To heal, to rise, to shine with radiant light.
My heart beats fierce, a drumbeat to the sky,
A monarch's wings, a symbol of my rebirth's sigh.

In this photo I stand, unbridled and free,
A testament to the power of faith's alchemy.

Angel Goddess Energy

On wings of white I rise, a spirit free,
Unshackled from the chains of disease's might,
My heart overflows with gratitude's sweet sea,
As I honor the angel goddess, shining bright.

With scars that tell the story of my hard-won fight,
I stand unashamed, in purity's white light,
My sheer lace robe, a symbol of my inner sight,
Reflecting the beauty that surrounds me, day and night.

In nature's hold, I find my peaceful nest,
The river's gentle flow, a soothing balm for my soul,
The greenery's vibrant hues, a testament to life's quest,
A celebration of my triumph, my spirit made whole.

With every breath, I thank the divine above,
For guiding me through darkness, to this radiant love.

Inner Wisdom

In the stillness of the night, I hear my soul's voice
A whispered truth that guides me to my heart's choice
A wisdom born, of intuition's gentle might
Illuminating my path, through life's plodding night

From Darkness to Light

In the shadowed recesses of my soul's dark night
A narrative of resilience slowly begins to take flight
A tapestry of transformation, woven from the threads of pain
A survivor's tale, of wounds that cut, but never took flight

The weight of family tragedy, a burden I did bear
A grief so profound, it threatened to consume me, to leave me bare
But in the darkness, a spark within me glowed
A light that flickered, yet never died, a light to guide me through

Through the crucible of suffering, I walked the narrow way
And found a strength I never knew I had, a brighter day
A sense of purpose, born of the ashes of my past
A radiant butterfly, emerging from the cocoon that would not last

In this journey from darkness to light, I found my voice, my song
A harmony of healing, that resonates all life long
A celebration of the human spirit, that never gives up the fight
A shining star that guides me through the darkest of nights.

Redemption's Song

My heart, once shattered by pain's relentless might
Now sings, with a voice redeemed, in the light of new sight
A song of hope, reborn in the fire of my soul
A melody of redemption, that forever will make me whole

In the depths of my being, a transformation took hold
A metamorphosis of spirit, where love did unfold
The shadows of my past, they faded into the light
As I emerged, reborn, in the radiance of divine sight

Through the crucible of suffering, I was refined and made new
My heart, once broken, now beats with a love that's pure and true
A love that echoes the divine, a harmony of the soul
A redemption song that whispers secrets of the universe's goal.

Queen of Angels, Blessed Mother Mary

In darkest hours, when mortal pain did reign
And sorrow's weight upon my soul did press
I sought the Mother, whose love doth sustain
And found solace in Mary's gentle caress

Her golden wings, a refuge from life's storm
Enfolded me, and soothed my troubled breast
As I, a child of sorrow, bled and mourned
She poured her love, and healed my deepest unrest

Like Christ, I too did bleed, and water flowed
In symbolic birth, my spirit was renewed
Through trials and tribulations, I've been led
To cling to Mary, my heart's steadfast creed

Now, in her loving light, I find my strength
And in her wings, a mother's love at length.

Grace and Peace Goddess Energy

As sunset's fiery hues upon me shine,
I bask in gratitude's gentle, warm space.
In the lake's stillness, I sit, heart and soul entwine,
Reflecting on blessings that fill every place.

Wet hair, bronzed skin, and soul afire,
I cherish this moment, pure and free.
In prayer pose, I honor life's desire,
To cherish each breath lightheartedly.

Gratitude's simplicity, I adore,
A feeling that fills my heart to the core.
In nature's splendor, I am made anew,
Reminded to thank life for all that's true.

In this pose, I embody grace and peace,
A goddess radiant, with heart that ceaselessly releases.

Gratitude's Garden

In Gratitude's Garden, where love's divine light shines
Lilies bloom, their pure white petals like angels' wings that entwine
Tulips sway, their cups of vibrant hue, like joyful trumpets' heavenly refrains
Gardenias unfold, their creamy blossoms like delicate, fragrant prayers that ascend

Roses entwine, their velvet softness like tender whispers of the soul
Hydrangeas burst, their blue and pink clusters like celestial showers that nourish me whole
In this sacred garden, I wander, free and light
Drinking in the beauty of each blossom's divine delight

The scent of blooming flowers fills my heart with reverence and peace
A sense of oneness with the universe's beauty, that forever releases
In Gratitude's Garden, I find my soul's true home
A place where love and joy forever roam, and I am never alone.

Love's Symphony

My heart, a symphony of love, plays on
A harmony of devotion that echoes all life long
A sacred refrain that whispers secrets of the soul
A celestial music, that makes my spirit whole

In every moment, I am orchestrated by love's design
A divine composition that weaves together heart and mind
The rhythm of my breath, the beat of my heart's drum
All blend in perfect harmony, a symphony that's never undone

The strings of compassion, the horns of joy and peace
The flutes of gentle whispers, the harps of heavenly release
All play their part in love's grand masterpiece
A majestic orchestration that echoes eternity

In this grand concerto, I find my soul's true home
A place where love and joy forever roam, and I am never alone
For in the music of love, I hear the divine
A celestial harmony that forever will be mine.

A Soul's Liberation

In the depths of my being, a truth I did find
A liberation from the chains of a toxic past entwined
A soul's awakening, where love and light did shine
And the weight of my mother's abuse, I could finally define

The memories of her words, they cut like a knife
The pain of her rejection, a wound that would not heal in life
But in the silence, I found my voice, my strength, my might
A resolve to rise above, to shine with a radiant light

In this journey of self-discovery, I found my way
Through the darkness of estrangement, to a brighter day
A day where I could stand tall, with a heart full of cheer
And know that I am worthy, despite the pain of the past year

So I spread my wings, and let the spirit lift me high
Above the hurt, above the pain, to a place where love does lie
Where the soul's liberation is a gift that's truly mine
A fortune that I cherish, a heart that's finally aligned.

The Weight of Legacy

In the garden of my soul, a tree of sorrow grew
Its roots a tangle of pain, its branches a legacy anew
A heritage of hurt, passed down through the years
A burden that I carried, through laughter and through tears

My mother's words, they whispered shame, they whispered blame
A toxic narrative that I internalized, that I could not reclaim
But as I walked the path of self-discovery and light
I saw the weight of legacy, and the chains that bound me tight

I realized that I am not the sum of my mother's fears
That I am a unique soul, with a story that's mine to clear
That the weight of legacy is a burden I can lay down
And rise above the pain, to a place where love does abound

So I let go of the past, and the hurt that it did bring
And I chose to forge a new path, where love and light do sing
A path that's mine alone, where I can walk with pride
And leave the weight of legacy, to wither and die.

A Heart's Forgiveness

In the stillness of my heart, a whisper echoed through
A call to forgiveness, a summons to let go, anew
A chance to release the pain, to heal the wounds of old
To find a sense of peace that would forever unfold

My mother's abuse, it left its scars, its marks on my soul
But as I walked the journey of healing and making whole
I saw that forgiveness is not for the one who did harm
But for the one who suffered, to find a sense of calm

Forgiveness is a choice, a decision to let go
To release the burden of resentment and anger's heavy toll
It's not forgetting, nor condoning, the pain of the past
But rising above it, to a place where love will forever last

So I chose to forgive, to let go of the pain
And find a sense of peace, that would forever remain
A heart's forgiveness, that set me free
A gift that I gave myself, a treasure that's mine to see.

Kuan Yin

In shattered depths, where heartache reigns supreme,
I seek Kuan Yin's compassion, pure and serene.
Estranged from blood ties, forged in painful dreams,
Abuse and sorrow's legacy, my heart's theme.

As a neurodivergent mind, once misunderstood,
Seizures mistaken for tantrums, childhood's mood.
Molested, betrayed by family's harmful hand,
And murder's stain, forever left to stand.

Yet in Kuan Yin's embrace, I find solace true,
Her energy flows, healing heart and soul anew.
Through her, forgiveness blooms, like lotus bright,
Peace settles, calming turbulent, darkest night.

With every breath, I let her love shine in,
And compassion's balm, my heart's wounds begin.

A Legacy of Love

In the sacred garden of my soul, a flower of forgiveness blooms
Petals of peace that unfold, like a lotus rising from the gloom
The fragrance of mercy wafts through the air, like incense sweet
As I release the burdens of resentment and anger's heavy weight

My children's laughter, a chorus of angels singing in harmony
A opus of joy that echoes through eternity
Their smiles, a reflection of the divine love that shines so bright
An illumination of hope that guides me through the darkest of nights

I forgave my abusers, as the Holy Spirit guided me to do
To release the chains of bondage, and walk in the light anew
As Yeshua taught me, to love and to forgive, to let go of the pain
And emerge, transformed and renewed, like a butterfly set free again

In this journey of forgiveness, I found a sense of spiritual peace
A oneness with the universe that my soul can't release
A legacy of love that I pass on to my children's hearts
A blessing that will forever be a work of art.

The Queen of Angels

In darkness, the Angelic Queen's radiance shines bright,
A shield of strength, protecting heart and light.
In 2018's gallbladder attack, I faced night,
Medically kidnapped, torn from love's warm sight.

Error and deceit led me to that grim place,
Where asylum walls confined my trembling space.
Yet, EMS angels intervened with grace,
Alerting my husband to the wrongful pace.

But even amid assault and cruel might,
The Angelic Queen's fierce power coursed through my being bright.
The psychiatrist saw truth, and I was free,
Released to loved ones, clinging to deity.

Now, as I heal, the Queen's protection stays,
Guarding my heart, guiding motherly ways.

From Darkness to Light

In the depths of darkness, I searched for the light
A guiding star, to lead me through the night
A voice within whispered words of hope and cheer
And I began to heal, to mend the tears

With every step I took, I left the shadows behind
And found my way, to a brighter state of mind
The darkness faded, as the light began to shine
And I emerged, whole and new, transformed by love's divine

Unshackling the Chains

In the depths of my prison, where pain and sorrow reign
I searched for the key, to unlock the chains that bound me in vain
A whispered promise of freedom's call
Echoed through my soul, and I began to hear the silence's fall

With every step I took, I found my way to break the chains
To unshackle the bonds, and to dance in wild, ecstatic refrains
The love and the light, they guided me through the night
And I emerged, radiant and bright, in the warm and golden light

In this journey of liberation, I found my way to the core
A freedom that healed the wounds, and soothed the heart's deep score
I learned to let go, to release the past
And I emerged, whole and new, like a bird set free at last

To rise above the pain, to find my way to the light
To heal, to mend, to soothe, and to take flight
Into the arms of love, where I am free to be
A soul unshackled, transformed, and set free.

A Heart's Transformation

In the depths of my heart, a metamorphosis took place
A transformation of love, that showed me a brand-new face
A reflection of kindness, of compassion and of light
A heart that was once broken, now healed and made right

With every step, I took, I found my way to love
To let go of the pain, and to rise above
The love and the light, they guided me through the night
And I emerged, whole and new, like a butterfly taking flight

In this journey of transformation, I found my way to the soul
A love that healed the wounds, and soothed the heart's deep role
I learned to forgive, to let go of the past
And I emerged, radiant and bright, like a phoenix rising at last

To rise above the pain, to find my way to the light
To heal, to mend, to soothe, and to take flight
Into the arms of love, where I am free to be
A heart transformed, renewed, and set free.

Into the Light

In the darkness of my past, I searched for the light
A guiding star, to lead me through the endless night
A whispered promise, of hope and redemption's call
Echoed through my soul, and I began to hear the silence's fall

With every step I took, I found my way to the threshold
A doorway to the light, where love and joy did unfold
The darkness faded, as the light began to shine
And I emerged, radiant and bright, like a soul reborn in love's divine

In this journey of illumination, I found my way to the core
A love that healed the wounds, and soothed the heart's deep score
I learned to let go, to release the past
And I emerged, whole and new, like a phoenix rising at last

To rise above the pain, to find my way to the light
To heal, to mend, to soothe, and to take flight
Into the arms of love, where I am free to be
A soul illuminated, transformed, and set free.

A Soul's Redemption

In the abyss of my darkness, where shadows danced and played
I searched for the light, a bonfire to guide me through the shades
A whispered promise, of hope and redemption's call
Echoed through my soul, and I began to hear the silence's fall

With every step I took, I left the chains of pain behind
And found my way, to a brighter state of mind
The darkness faded, as the light began to seep
And I emerged, transformed, like a soul reborn in love's sweet keep

In this journey of redemption, I found my way to the divine
A love that healed the wounds, and soothed the heart's deep mine
I learned to forgive, to let go of the past
And I emerged, radiant and bright, like a morning sunrise that will forever last

To transcend the shadows, to ascend to love's pure light
To restore, to renew, to revive, and to take gentle flight
Into the arms of love, where I am free to be
A soul redeemed.

A Soul's Courage

In realms of darkness, where shadows roam
My soul stood tall, a guiding light to call home
The courage and strength, that lay within my heart
Guided me through trials, and never did depart

Through labyrinths of pain, I navigated with ease
A warrior of light, who faced my deepest freeze
The violations of my past, the wounds that would not heal
Could not diminish my spirit, my soul's unyielding zeal

Like a radiant sun, I emerged from the darkest night
A golden butterfly, with wings that bore my name in light
My energy, a balm, that heals the deepest scar
A testament to my strength, a shining star

In my journey, I found hope, a radiant light to guide my way
To gather my courage, to face a brand-new day.

A Dreamer's Faith

My heart beats with a dreamer's fire
A passion that burns bright, a soul that aspires
To create a world where love and joy entwine
A heaven on earth, where hearts can heal and align

Through trials and tribulations, I held on to faith
A lifeline that guided me, through life's turbulent wave
The murder of my father, the battle with disease
Could not shake my conviction, my spirit's release

Like a lotus blooming, I rose above the pain
A golden butterfly, with wings that shone like rain
My energy, a gift, that heals the deepest wound
A testament to my faith, a love that's unbound

In my journey, I found strength, a guiding force to lead my way
To hold on to faith, to face a brand-new day.

A Healer's Heart

My soul is a sanctuary, a haven of peace
A place where hearts can heal, where love and joy release
My energy, a balm, that soothes the deepest scar
A gift from the universe, a love that's my star

As a holistic practitioner, I weave a tapestry of love
A healing art that mends the heart, and sends it soaring above
My presence, a blessing, a gift to all who meet
A golden butterfly, with wings that touch the heart's sweet seat

Through my journey, I found hope, a shining light to guide my way
To heal, to mend, to soothe, and to seize a brand-new day
My heart, a sanctuary, a haven of peace and love
A place where we can heal, and rise above

In my energy, I find solace, a comfort that's real
A love that heals, a heart that feels.

A Golden Butterfly Soul

My soul is a golden butterfly, with wings that shine so bright
A radiant presence, a guiding force, that leads us through the darkest night
My energy, a gift, that heals the deepest wound
A love that's pure, a heart that's sound

From the ashes of my past, I emerged anew
A warrior of light, who faced my deepest pains and broke through
My journey, a testament to my strength and my might
A golden butterfly, who shines with love and light

In my presence, you find peace, a sense of calm and rest
A love that heals, a heart that's blessed
My soul, a sanctuary, a haven of peace and love
A place where we can heal, and rise above

In my golden butterfly soul, you find your way
To heal, to mend, to soothe, and to seize a brand-new day.

Golden Wings

From ashes of tragedy, I rose anew,
A firebird reborn, with heart still aglow.
Cancer's dark shadow could not break me through,
For I am a warrior, with spirit that glows.

My family's memory lives on in my soul,
Their love and legacy forever whole.
I wear my wings, a symbol of my might,
Golden and strong, shining with inner light.

With every breath, I claim my freedom true,
Unshackled from pain, my spirit anew.
I stand on this rock, with waters cascading free,
A testament to the power that's been in me.

My wings envelop me, a shield and a guide,
Reminding me of the strength I have inside.

Sunny

www.ingramcontent.com/pod-product-compliance
Lightning Source LLC
Chambersburg PA
CBHW041427120626
46547CB00002B/119